CW00506560

CAPE TOWN TRAVEL GUIDE

All rights reserved. No part of this publication may be reproduced, distributed, or transmitted in any form or by any means, including photocopying, recording, or other electronic or mechanical methods, without the prior written permission of the publisher, except in the case of brief quotations embodied in critical reviews and certain other noncommercial uses permitted by copyright law.

Copyright © Mildred T. Ward, 2023.

Table of content

Introduction
History Of Cape Town

Section 1
What To Expect In Cape Town

Section 2
Getting Around In Cape Town

Section 3
Things To Do in Cape Town

Section 4
The Best Areas To Stay In Cape Town

Section 5
Where To Eat

Section 6
Ways to Save Money While Visiting Cape Town

Section 7
Travel cape town on a budget

Introduction

History Of Cape Town

One of South Africa's most historically significant cities is Cape Town. The primary European colonists entered South Africa here, at the Mother City, which also marked the beginning of the slave trade in the country. Nelson Mandela, who was executed on the tiny

Robben Island in Table Bay, was perhaps the most well-known political prisoner in the whole world when incarcerated there. The following are a few of the historical moments that helped shape Cape Town into what it is today.

The Sea gave rise to Table Mountain.

Table Mountain was by no means a mountain thousands of years ago, during the Karoo Ice Period. Although it was at sea level, what was there was a foundation of rocks and layers of sandstone. The ice and tension from the underlying magma combined to harden the top layer, producing the renowned level piece that we can still see today. The city's famous landmark was gradually forced to climb as the landmasses were destroyed and influenced, and it currently stands a kilometer tall while oblivious to the road.

Table Mountain as seen from Camps Bay

Could you believe the very extreme age of the Table Mountain Ethereal Cableway? Before it, the only way to reach the peak of the mountain was on foot, and only the most adventurous or courageous had done so. The first cable car chugged its way to the top on October 4, 1929, after two years of difficult and dangerous construction, laden with energized and probably quite frightened passengers. Since then, it has undergone several redesigns, and today's ascent is going quite well.

Initial Capetonians

Before the majority of European settlers arrived, the Khoisan people called Table Mountain and the surrounding area home. They named the city Hui!Gaeb, they were gifted, creative people who possessed a wealth of knowledge about the native flora and wildlife. Hoerikwaggo, or "Mountain in the sea," was also given as Table Mountain's initial name.

European Habitation

After moving the Cape by ship in the latter half of the 1400s, the Portuguese explorer

Bartolomeu Dias became the first European to view what is now Cape Town. Nonetheless, Dutch colonist, Jan van Riebeeck became the first European to visit its grave in 1652. The Dutch East India Company (VOC) dispatched him to set up an inventory station for ships sailing from Europe to India.

Shortly after Van Riebeeck established the inventory station, the VOC imported slaves from Singapore, Malaysia, and Indonesia to work on the farms that produced the green vegetables for passing ships. This brought assurance to our shining beaches, coupled with cape food.

Pilgrim ping pong

Since it was originally settled in 1652, Cape Town has alternated between the British and the Dutch, two of the greatest frontier powers of the era. The Dutch were in authority for the primary century and a half after settlement. Although taking control in 1795, England ultimately lost it to the Dutch in 1803. It took another three years for the Cape to return to

British control, where it stayed for the ensuing century and a half. South Africa was finally granted freedom in the middle of the twentieth century, but it took an additional 90 years before the key majority rule decisions were made.

Noon gun

The oldest ritual in Cape Town is still in good shape and routinely surprises visitors at precisely noon. A shot from an ancient gun is fired from Signal Hill's highest point, resonating throughout the Downtown. At first, it was designed to announce oncoming ships and alert vendors that it was time to bring their wares into the harbor. The gun has been firing since about 1806, and a backup gun is always available in case the first one doesn't work. According to legend, the weapon only exploded once during those two centuries as a result of a flaw that made the remote sign sluggish.

Evacuation and successful return

District Six's once-raucous creative hub on the fringes of the city gained notoriety for some unpleasant reasons. At than 60,000 residents of the clamoring area were relocated during the 1970s under the then-politically-sanctioned system of racial segregation to various areas outside the 'white' metropolis. Yet in 1990, Nelson Mandela gave his first speech after being released from the Robben Island prison from the Hall gallery, just two blocks from District 6 and the City.

Section 1

I had the good fortune to spend roughly seven days discovering Cape Town's charms on my first vacation to the continent of Africa. The next year, I ended up relocating to Cape Town, where I spent more than a year. The beachside city offers a wide range of activities for people of all ages thanks to its mouthwatering cuisine and stunning natural surroundings. It is a multicultural city with thriving nightlife, bistro culture, and a wealth of historical landmarks.

What To Expect In Cape Town

Language:

South Africa guarantees an astounding eleven official languages, however the most well-known you'll hear in and around Cape Town is English — the language of business and media — followed by Afrikaans and Xhosa in the city.

Currency:

The currency in South Africa is known as a Rand.

Credit cards and Banks:

Most retailers and cafés acknowledge debit cards as payment.

Climate:

Humidity is very low in Cape Town, so while the summers are warm, they aren't excessively damp. Wintertime, be that as it may, is crisp with the ocean winds blowing in from the southeast. The best times to visit are the cusp months, October and November, springtime in South Africa, or from December to February when the days are at their longest and hottest. Winter from June to August will in general be rainy and cold.

Section 2

Getting Around In Cape Town

There are perhaps one or two ways for getting around Cape Town, contingent on your budget and needs. If you're going on a strict spending plan, the most ideal choice is to utilise the bus system. Bus tickets are somewhat cheap, and you can use them to get around the city without any problem. The MyCiTi bus system is solid, protected, and proficient. There are additionally Uber or metered taxis that can be flagged down from the road.

If you have a bit more cash to spend, you should consider hiring a vehicle. This can be an extraordinary choice if you're going with a group of people, as it will permit you to part with the expense of fuel and parking. Vehicle hire organisations as a rule have great rates for the week-by-week or month-to-month rentals, so it's most certainly worth considering on the off chance that you're anticipating staying in Cape Town for some time.

If you're searching for the least expensive choice, a bike is the best approach. You can undoubtedly travel all over without stressing over stopping or traffic. Simply try to carry a map with you so you don't get lost!

CAB OR TAXI

There are countless metered taxis accessible. It's not difficult to track down one close to significant attractions or at the airport.

CAR HIRE

Every one of the significant organisations works out of the airport and has city depots. Gas stations accept both cash and credit, yet not all. There will be a sign outside telling you on the off chance that they acknowledge credit or not, yet it's really smart to constantly have some money on you for good measure. You will likewise require little change for tolls on major roads.

BICYCLE

Cape Town has turned into a very bicycle well-disposed city, with committed bicycle paths in many regions and a portion of the world's greatest cycle races facilitated here. Cycling in Cape Town isn't just a tomfoolery and solid game — it can likewise be a great method for getting around the city.

TRAIN

Trains run basic worker courses into the city and loosen up along the picturesque Southern line, which extends as far as Simon's Town. It is an affordable choice to go around the city.

MINIBUS TAXI

To travel like a local, jump on a minibus taxi for a memorable ride. They can be found on main streets and centre points like Cape Town Railroad Stations' rooftops and at taxi positions in suburbia and municipalities. Charges are reasonable and you get on or off where you need. Expect local kwaito to be booming and the 'gaatjie' (articulated gaa-chi), or door operator, to be prepared with astute editorial.

BUS

Cape Town has various confidential bus organisations and passenger bus services, as well as the City Touring bus. The City Touring Bus is a great method for seeing the city at your speed as you bounce on and off at your leisure. The MyCiti bus is one more speedy and simple method for getting around the city and encompasses.

UBER

Uber is one of the most amazing ways of getting around Cape Town. The distances between a large portion of the top attractions are short, making it a savvy choice for your trip. You can likewise demand a ride from Cape Town International Air terminal by utilising the free wireless internet.

MY CITI BUS

One more reasonable method for getting around the city is with the My CitiBus service. You can purchase a transport code from one of the stations and top it up as you go. There is a free application that you can download that rundowns the schedules for each stop, passages, and a course organiser.

RENT A SCOOTER

Scooters and Vespas are extremely famous in Cape Town. They're an exceptionally quick and helpful method for getting around, simply make sure to wear your helmet!

Section 3

Things To Do in Cape Town

Sir Francis Drake described this region of the planet many years ago as "the most lovely Cape in all the bounds of the world," and that description still holds today. In addition to its natural splendor, Cape Town is admired and revered for its extensive history and diverse socioeconomic makeup. Its reputation as one of the world's premier gastronomic destinations further adds to its attractiveness.

In light of this, the list of events below highlights many aspects of this vibrant metropolis. These are the things you should do in Cape Town, whether you're looking for exciting outdoor activities, exquisite gourmet experiences, or an explosion of creativity.

Do a sunset cruise

For quintessential Cape Town sundowners, jump on board Investigate or level of intelligence, extravagance teak-decked sailboats to watch the sun go down. Lean back on the trampolines in front, or loosen up on agreeable cushion seating and make certain to have a camera prepared, as the journey offers dazzling perspectives on the city with Table Mountain as its setting. The yacht leaves from the Waterfront and heads out into Table Bay and along the Atlantic Seaboard, returning an hour and a half later... to see the primary stars show up and the moon ascend in the smooth blue sky.

Cruise the coast on a Whiteboard

It's similar to surfing, however more hi-tech... and could we add less difficulty. Electric hydrofoils are essentially surfboards with an electric propeller connected to an enormous blade, that permits a foiler to ride over the water - or "fly" (to utilise the language). It requires about 90 minutes to get familiar with everything - you'll be provided with a wetsuit, cap, and life vest, and after a short introduction and security preparation, head into the water for your example with the master.

All of a sudden, you'll be standing up, cruising, and cutting over the sea on your emanation-free Fliteboard. When you understand what you're doing, you can require two-hour directed voyages through the shore.

Aquatic fun at Elgin River Lodge

If a laidback day close to a river seems like your concept of flawlessness, make a beeline for this apple ranch in the Elgin Valley. With 2.5km of Palmiet River frontage, it's an astonishing aquatic jungle gym for the young and youthful on a fundamental level.

There's swimming, tubing, kayaking, a slide into the water, barge travels, a slip 'n slide, water-skiing, and wakeboarding... in addition to climbing and biking trails over the 100-hectare property, and a games room with table tennis, darts, and a pool table. The enchanting toad on the River bar supplies refreshments, or partake in a picnic.

Kayak along the Atlantic Seaboard

Rowing on the vast sea inspires a feeling of freedom and adventure. This two-hour directed kayaking trip leaves from Three Anchor Bay beach beneath the Sea Point Promenade and ventures along the Sea Point shoreline toward Bantry Bay or, in the other course, into Table Bay and towards the V&A Waterfront -

contingent upon the climate and your inclination.

You'll journey past wrecks and dolphins, maybe experiencing penguins, seals, and sunfish. Besides, you'll get to see what the city and its magnificent mountains look like from the ocean. The Nightfall Experience adds the radiant skyscapes of sundowner time.

Swim at Silvermine

Under an hour's drive from the city centre, this enormous, flickering, peak reservoir is effectively open to everybody and is tremendously famous for comfortable swims and picnics. The water is somewhat warmer than the ocean, and there's a one-kilometre boardwalk trail around the dam (wheelchair and pram cordial). It's additionally the beginning stage for different hikes, the most well-known of which are Elephant's Eye Cave, Silvermine Edge, and Sentinel View.

SUP around the Waterfront

Stand-up paddleboarding (SUPing) has seen an upsurge in fame throughout the last ten years and assuming you might want to take a shot at it, make a beeline for the Waterfront. The quiet, sans-wave channels are the ideal preparation ground for wannabe SUPers. You'll be furnished with all the stuff and start preparation - anticipate a couple of tumbles into the shallow water - and whenever you've excelled at adjusting on the load up, now is the right time to set off on a three-kilometre circle of the waterways.

Would it be a good idea for you to require it, an aide will go with you; on the off chance that you know how to SUP, you can lease a board and journey the waterways, or lease one for an end-of-the-week getaway.

Learn how to surf at Muizenberg

Surfing devotees will let you know there could be no more prominent method for de-stressing than to be in the sea, riding the waves. These pleasant examples will make them familiar with the rudiments in the blink of an eye. All you want to bring is a swimming outfit, towel, sunscreen, and excitement.

All expertise levels and ages are gladly received; amateur and transitional level surfers will want to calibrate their board abilities in gathering or confidential examples, while under-10s get one-on-one illustrations.

Visit African Seaforest

African Seaforest is a submerged wonderland of giant, influencing bamboo kelp, home to myriad animals, of all shapes and sizes (counting cow sharks, feline sharks, crevasse sharks - and octopuses). Submerge yourself in this world on a directed scuba-jumping journey at Pyramid Rock and Partridge Point in False Bay.

The most extreme profundity is 12 metres, which makes for extraordinary permeability and a decent decision for novice jumpers. The outing is likewise accessible as a swimming encounter, where inquisitive, fun-loving seals play with swimmers on a superficial level. A while later, anticipate a hot shower and lunch.

Coasteering in False Bay

If sunning yourself on the beach or swimming on the shore is somewhat manageable for your preferences, what about a privateer-style coastline experience? You'll advance along a part of the False Bay shoreline, swimming, snorkelling, rock-scrambling, and leaping off stones into the water - all while getting up near the marine life (and a couple of penguins) in the more stunning segments of the cove.

Think kloofing or canyoning, however in an ocean environment. All wellness and expertise levels are gladly received, as you're joined by an aide and outfitted with a PFD (personal flotation device) and helmet. A wetsuit and booties can be leased.

Mountain ziplining in Elgin

Take off Tarzan-style through an aerial jungle gym of fynbos, Forest, magnificent gorges, and roaring waterfalls on this zipline experience. Situated in the Hottentots-Holland Nature Reserve, the Cape Canopy visit has opened up beforehand distant pieces of this rocky wilderness.

Everything starts with a 4×4, enjoying some real success in the mountains, where visitors are joined to links that run from one stage to another, and directed by proficient aides. There are 11 slides altogether - the longest is 320 metres. At a certain point, you'll likewise stroll across an engineered overpass that traverses a magnificent twofold cascade.

Paraglide over Sea Point

Experience Cape Town's grandness from as high as possible - and get your adrenaline syphoning - on one of these couple undertakings. No information or experience of paragliding is vital - your instructor will go through the rules and clasp you in safely, and you'll be joined by a specialist pilot. Once in the air, you should simply take a load off as you get a seagull's perspective on the city, floating at around 40 km/h, to your last objective on the Sea Point Promenade.

Flights last somewhere in the range of five and 30 minutes, contingent upon the breeze; in wonderful weather patterns, your pilot will tell you the best way to direct so you can fly the paraglider yourself!

Scooter down Table Mountain

You might have strolled the ways of Table Mountain ordinarily, yet have you at any point done it on a freewheeler? The marvellous view is even more strengthening during a rough terrain experience, particularly when you get to feel a surge of adrenaline as you whizz down slants.

The two-hour visit starts at the highest point of Signal Hill for your most memorable downhill rush to Bo-Kaap, then continues toward the lower slants of Table Mountain, from which you slide through Deer Park.

The bikes are non motorised yet incredibly steady (they're utilised to explore the inclines of the Swiss Alps during summer, all things considered), making for a family-accommodating and eco-accommodating experience.

Heli-trekking in Jonkershoek

Feel like an action hero as you get raced off in a helicopter to be dropped in the mountains to hit some wonderful biking trails. The Hottentots-Holland mountain range is bungled by 18 MTB trails taking special care of differing wellness and ability levels.

Whether you're searching for a novice accommodating ride or a rough experience, you'll get glorious perspectives on Stellenbosch. A heli-drop (in a helicopter with unique bicycle racks!) implies you have new legs to capitalise on the trekking. An accomplished aide is incorporated, and the people who don't want to bicycle can pick one of the many climbing trails all things being equal.

Visit the penguins at Boulders beach

Boulders beach is perhaps one of the most popular beaches in Cape Town, on account of its occupant African penguins. It's one of only a handful of exceptional spots in existence where you can get up near these characterful yet jeopardised birds - and even swim with them. The settlement falls under the security of SANParks and requires a protection expense to get entrance. When there, you can watch the penguins float through the water like torpedoes and waddle about ashore.

Further along, the footpath from the ocean side itself is the super-safeguarded province, where many birds assemble and settle. The immaculate oceanside itself (which is very protected from wind areas of strength) offers incredible sandcastle building, swimming, stone jumping, and picnics.

Babylonstoren garden visit

This superb 5-hectare legacy garden around which all else flows is a wonder to see. Propelled by the first food nurseries of the Cape's initial days, a confounding assortment of plants is developed. It's partitioned into 15 expansive regions, with segments for vegetables, natural products, spices, honey bees, organic product trees, and numerous others of verifiable and herbal importance, as well as native plants, blossoms, and a thorny pear labyrinth.

Along the way, you'll see ducks, chickens, turtles, and jackasses and that's only the tip of the iceberg. You can float through and find it all alone (kids love sprinkling in the water highlights), or take a direct visit with the landscapers, who will urge you to smell, contact, pick and taste the occasional abundance. There are additionally unique assortments of succulents, cycads, and therapeutic plants and that's only the tip of the iceberg.

Explore Kirstenbosch

Established in 1913 to save the Cape's uncommonly widely varied vegetation, the 36-hectare Kirstenbosch Public Greenhouse is famous for its magnificence and variety. Arranged on the southern slants of Table Mountain, the nurseries are home to an assortment of verdure (north of 7 000 species), native birds, and creatures, making it an unwinding (and instructive) outing for all. It's unspoiled for beautiful walks around quiet encompasses, with the Boomslang Overhang Walk an unmistakable feature for those perspectives!

You'll find Colonel Water basin, the Garden of Weeds, the Garden of Extinction, the vlei, and cycad woods, to give some examples of delights. Pack a cookout hamper (or request one from the lunch nook) and get comfortable for the day, while the children wander indiscriminately, investigating streams, climbing rocks, and partaking in the vast expanses.

Cape Point

With plenty of activities and sea, Cape Point Nature Save is a superb road trip objective for local people and sightseers. Find the rich history of the region at the guest's middle, partake in an ocean-side walk and swim in the lagoons at Buffels Narrows, or go out on a more brave climb (where you could experience some natural life-like buck or ostriches).

Get the Flying Dutchman funicular at Cape Highlight visit the beacon or valiant the lofty moves toward finding shocking Diaz Beach.

Visit Stellenbosch vineyards

Rather than simply looking at those grape plantations, you can coast through the columns of vines and around the ranch and gardens at Spier Estate on a two-wheeled PT (individual carrier). You'll make significantly more progress than by walking, while at the same time partaking in the perspectives and learning a few fascinating things about biodynamic cultivation.

Before you start your ride, a 20-minute instructional course will prepare you. There are choices regardless of wine sampling, as well as heartfelt later visits that incorporate a container of wine for two to share and the delightful light and shadows of sundown hour.

A Visit to the Two Oceans Aquarium

This top-notch aquarium is home to more than 8 000 sea creatures of all shapes, sizes, and varieties - including clownfish (hello Nemo!). It's a thrilling look into life off our shores, with entrancing influencing kelp timberland, schools of sparkling fish swimming as one, skimming turtles, and even sharks, which can likewise be seen from inside a 10-metre glass burrow.

There are more intriguing fish, as well, like jams, octopuses, seahorses, pufferfish, and moray eels. The well-known penguin show is generally a hit. A fantastical submerged wonderland's continually changing, in addition to children can get up near anemones and starfish at the Touch Pool. There are additionally marine-themed manikin shows and expressions and artworks for youngsters.

The V&A Waterfront

This environmental, humming working harbour in the focal point of Cape Town is an objective of its own doing, with many energising attractions that make local people and travellers want more and more. Aside from the Two Oceans Aquarium, kids (and grown-ups) will cherish the Cape Wheel - incredible 40-metre-high perspectives and a thrilling ride; the cavern putt and a boat stumble on Steamboat Vicky or the privateer transport.

Hang out at Kalk Bay Harbor

The well-known red-and-white-striped lighthouse at the tip of a clamouring dock is one of the getting-through pictures of Kalk Bay. A famous spot for an afternoon wander during summer, in winter the harbour sheds its laidback picture and shines a different light on the expression "Cape of Storms", as enormous waves run into the pier and beacon.

Yet, most days, this is a charming spot - you'll experience occupant perky seals, stealing seagulls and bright characters, have the option to purchase new off-the-boat fish to bring back home for supper, and enjoy probably the best-fried fish and French fries around at one of the pleasant harbourside restaurants.

Visit Wonderdal at Hazendal

Wonderdal is an exceptional, cutting-edge edutainment community mixing imaginative plans and top-notch tech in a vivid and intelligent space. As they explore, kids are joined by the Amuki, the virtual occupants of Wonderdal.

These cordial, idiosyncratic animals will direct them through the experience, giving them tips on the best way to finish the exercises and undertakings themed around science, nature, and fundamental abilities. The 1 000m2 space is access-controlled and administered consistently, so guardians are allowed to proceed to partake in different pursuits for which Hazendal is known (the Babushka Store, wine sampling, high tea, picnics and that's only the tip of the iceberg).

Explore Pearly Beach

For an equine encounter that is however elating as it could be lovely, go to Pearly Beach (simply past Gansbaai). As you jog close to the bluest ocean on the best white sand, guide Sarah Coronaios will go with you while her better half, Kos, catches the second in pictures or on GoPro or drone video. The 2.5-hour trails are reasonable for all degrees of riders, and tenderfoots are gladly received and urged to encounter an ocean side ride - with a potential swim in the water with the thoroughly prepared ponies. Different choices incorporate a ride at nightfall, a ride with a celebratory glass of effervescent, and an inland mountain fynbos trail in winter.

Visit the Norval Art Foundation

This family-accommodating safe house of art and nature in the peaceful Constantia Winelands needs time to be valued, so make a day of it. Inside the Norval Foundation's motivation-planned straight structure you'll find a series of displays and a bundle of art exhibitions exhibiting top South African and African current workmanship - going from huge scope establishments to films.

Outside is an intuitive figure garden amid native greenery, a stretch of wetlands, clearing perspectives on grape plantations and the South Promontory past, an amphitheatre, a kids' jungle gym, and exquisite cookout spots. The Skotnes Restaurant and Bar includes a bistro-style menu and outside tables.

Movies under the stars

Watch your #1 flick at The Galileo Open Air Cinema's areas around Cape Town and the Winelands. Not exclusively will you be blessed to receive a family hit, faction #1, romcom, or blast from the past, yet it's a great method for going through a night! You'll have the choice of requesting snacks - like popcorn, desserts, and drinks - when you book your tickets online or purchase food like burgers, pizzas, and shawarmas from the merchants at the scene. There is likewise a bar for brews, wine, and effervescent. Find a spot on the yards and settle in - ticket choices incorporate backrests and covers.

Visit Zeitz MOCAA

Promoted as Cape Town's own special Tate Modern, the Zeitz MOCAA (Museum of Contemporary Art Africa) is plain to see. Situated in 56 previous grain silos in the harbour, the eight-story space went through a best-in-class change in 2017. Aside from the wonderful design, it houses 6 000m2 of presentation space with exhibitions on each floor displaying the state of the artwork. The numerous and fluctuating spaces incorporate the house of prayer like a Chamber, Places for Ensemble, Photography, and The Moving Image, a roof design garden, and a shop supplied with arty things. The Ocular Lounge is an incredible spot for dinner and drinks with impressive perspectives.

Section 4

The Best Areas To Stay In Cape Town

When you first arrive in a new place, it can be challenging to predict what to expect. It might be difficult to choose a place to stay in Cape Town, especially without local expertise. Read on to learn more about the personalities of each place as we have access to local knowledge of vast quantities at once.

Bo-Kaap

The Bo-Kaap is found simply up the slope from the City Bowl, and it's frequently alluded to as the Malay Quarter. It's known for its rich history and bright houses lining cobbled roads. A significant number of the inhabitants are decedents of the liberated slaves who initially settled in the region, and it's genuinely Cape Town.

City Bowl

The City Bowl itself is a decent decision for those who like to be part of the activity. You'll be near syphoning clubs and bars, and there are phenomenal eateries everywhere. There are upmarket hotels, divey inns, boutique backpackers, and essentially every other sort of accommodation you can envision. It's a clamouring cosmopolitan blend, and there's truly something for everybody. There are heaps of buses, cabs, trains, and Ubers around to get you from A to B.

Woodstock

Woodstock has turned into a centre point for artists and business entrepreneurs as of late. This is where you'll find numerous youthful experts, international students, new companies, and independent ventures. It's likewise an old area of the city, and there is a different blend of individuals who call the region home. It's truly near the city, however somewhat more affordable to stay in. It's on the suburbanite courses, so there is more than adequate modest transport, although it's not generally as protected as the tourist centre points.

V&A Waterfront

The Waterfront, while not, in fact, an area, is a centre of movement where you'll track down upmarket lodgings, eateries, and bars generally helpfully in a similar spot. It's generally protected, and you'll have the option to stroll to tourist destination flight focuses. It's additionally home to the Aquarium, and the Robben Island Museum, and is the principal stop on the City Touring bus courses. Accommodation here isn't cheap, however, it's destined to be of an elevated requirement.

De Waterkant

De Waterkant is a popular little town, likewise bearing the city. It has a cutting-edge feel, with craftsman shops and fabulous little restaurants and bars.

Sea Point

The Sea Point promenade, which extends for a few kilometres along the Atlantic Ocean, is maybe Sea Point's most well-known milestone, alongside its public pool at the Bantry Bay end. The Main Street is thick with restaurants serving worldwide cooking - Greek, Italian, and a wide range of Asian - as well as bars, watering openings, and shops. It's a rural area loaded up with character and peculiarity, and it's likewise where you'll track down various extraordinary gay bars and clubs.

Green Point

Green Point is Sea Point's more upmarket neighbour, and the oceanfront Main Street is fixed with loft blocks. This is where the Cape Town Stadium is found, so it's an extraordinary decision on the off chance that you're visiting the area for games or huge shows. It's likewise near the dazzling seashores of the Atlantic Seaboard.

Clifton and Camps Bay

These sister areas are to a great extent composed of gaudy houses and manors ignoring the Atlantic Ocean. This is where you'll track down the whole of Cape Town, and where VIPs frequently decide to Stay. However, try not to let that put you off: it's not difficult to imagine tracking down generally reasonable accommodation here, and justified for the perspectives alone. The seashores are frequently occupied, and for good reason. The sea on this side of the mountain is cool, yet the wide, sandy seashores make for fantastic sun-washing, volleyball, and people-watching.

Hout Cove

Hout Cove is around 20-30 minutes from the city, between the Atlantic Seaboard and Noordhoek. It has an ocean-side town feel, however, is somewhat more of a centre point than the Deep South. It's on the City Touring Blue Course, so investigating the city from here is conceivable. The ocean side is exquisite, and there are numerous restaurants, an exuberant end-of-the-week market, and a couple of bars.

Muizenberg

Muizenberg is the old dam of the False Bay shoreline. It's something like 15-20 minutes from the city, and there are a couple of public transport choices. The long, sandy ocean side is famous for neighbourhood surfers, and it has a surfer-town feel to it. There are surf shops, easygoing bars, and restaurants right close to the ocean side, which is fixed with authoritative beautiful ocean-side cabins.

Kalk Bay

Kalk Bay is a fishing town at heart, with an energetic harbour in its middle. There are numerous little store shops, selling clothes, collectibles, and knickknacks. This is where you'll discover the absolute best seafood around, and the speed of life is slow.

It's a decent base to explore the South, including Cape Point, and a phenomenal spot to remain if you have any desire to meet the educated and bohemian local people, yet it is somewhat distant from the City Bowl.

Observatory

Obs, as it's known locally, is a genuine mixture of people. It's a bohemian exploring centre point, and a large portion of the accommodation accessible is reasonable and clamouring hostels. You'll track down loads of aesthetic shops, stores with classic and surprising apparel, and well-being food stores.

There are likewise many bars and restaurants providing food for all preferences, offering an energetic nightlife scene that happens until the early morning. The observatory is on all the vitally open transport courses and is under six kilometres from the City Bowl-around a 10-minute drive beyond heavy traffic.

Newlands

Newlands is very different in what it offers, with beguiling little town-style malls, steakhouses, bars, restaurants, and lovely woods and streams. It's relatively near the city centre area, however well beyond the rushing about. If you're searching for a tranquil guest house, BnB, Airbnb, or hotel, this is a decent spot to base yourself. It is likewise home to the Newlands Stadium, so it's a well-known decision for those going to games.

Khayelitsha

Khayelitsha is Cape Town's biggest township, and it's a decent spot to remain on the off chance that you're after truly reasonable homestays in the "genuine", legitimate Cape Town. There is a lot to do here, and as long as you pay attention to your hosts and utilise solid, licensed transport suppliers, it's safe to visit.

Somerset West

Somerset West is around 30 minutes to an hour outside Cape Town, in the core of the Helderberg Wine Course. There are numerous hotels, BnBs, and guest houses to remain in, to suit most spending plans. It's somewhat distant from the actual city, yet offers simple admittance to the Winelands. Remain here for high-end food and wine sampling.

Durbanville

Durbanville is underrated as a spot to stay. It's a fair drive beyond the city, yet it offers unbelievable mountain perspectives and clearing grape plantations. The Durbanville Wine Course has a few fabulous domains, with extraordinary restaurants.

Bloubergstrand

Bloubergstrand is where you'll find the image postcard perspective on Table Mountain across the water. Accommodation here is essentially hotels and resorts, and the seashores are exceptionally famous. It's likewise the kitesurfing capital of Cape Town, so on the off chance that watersports are your scene don't miss it!

Where To Eat

FYN

A 50-seater urban eatery; The menu (and stylistic layout) is African-motivated, with an overall Japanese style, making for an enchanting (and delightful) mix of tastes, flavours, surfaces, and styles.

FYN's speedy inner city illuminates the menu - a dense five-course kaiseki-style insight - with probably the most unique wine pairings, and politeness of Jennifer (who burned through 17 years at La Colombe as sommelier and supervisor). Bravo!

Concerning the setting, the restaurant roosts on the fifth floor, bragging high as can be seen Table Mountain and Lion's Head. The insides are modern, warm, and authorised, with the kitchen in the focal point of the space.

Pier Waterside New

The freshest expansion to Scot Kirton's restaurant empire isn't "simply one more" La Colombe experience. Pier guarantees culinary experience and vain behaviours, true to form, yet with John Norris-Rogers in control, the attention is obviously on the best flavours cajoled from the best local produce. On offer is a bunch of 9 or 11 dishes going through the test of endurance of the La Colombe group's abilities easily - from the absolute first "nibble" to the petit fours presented with the bill.

Thali

This interesting Indian-tapas restaurant is an instance of the more (dishes you share), the merrier. The well-known Tapas for Two, contains eight dishes, including sambals, poppadoms, and tandoor, finishing in the greatest curries that, joined with the extraordinary inside stylistic layout and lighting, will move you to the fragrant roads of Delhi.

Chefs Warehouse Beau Constantia

The delightful sister to the outstanding Chefs Warehouse Pinchos and Wine Bar in the downtown area, this hummed-about restaurant offers a set menu of top-notch food type global tapas, conveyed with superb perspectives across the popular vine-clad valley.

It has prepared a tasty exhibit of creative dishes with an accentuation on newly reaped produce from the homestead's nurseries, and an infusion of Southeast Asian flavours. Combined with the dazzling setting, stylish interior, and all-encompassing vistas, this is a feasting experience worth thinking of as home.

Beyond

The kitchen delivers a compelling lineup of pitch-perfect à la carte dishes that are pared-back and accessible. Nab a vineyard-facing table and make sure Jennifer keeps topping you up with the 2019 chardonnay – intoxicatingly fragrant; one would love to spray it all over one's body.

Salsify

Ignoring a dazzling stretch of the Atlantic Ocean in a verdant pocket of Camps Bay, Salsify at The Roundhouse. A sign of approval for its sea-confronting setting - fish features conspicuously on the menu, capably and delicately ready.

Each dish is a smaller-than-expected wonder: refined, practical cooking at its unshowy best. The interior, as well, is perfect: a reasonable blend of restless complexity, with cutting-edge craftsmanship set against extravagant textures and goods. Also, as you'd expect, service is praiseworthy.

Homespun by Matt

The genuine front way to this Blouberg area of interest opens onto a drape - a so-called gateway, maybe - that protects the dull and comfortable restaurant from the bustling road. Candelabra and darkened copper-pipe lights set a romantic state of mind; liners and placemats produced using wooden beds sit on uncovered wooden tables - an informal environment for the connoisseur venture that takes burger joints from Europe to Asia and home once more.

The five-course tasting menu with wine pairings starts with Matt's contort on ceviche served in a bed of steaming shells.

La Colombe

High up on the slants of the Constantiaberg mountains, Silvermist Wine Estate is a genuine gem in the Constantia Wine Valley's crown. The trendy restaurant's pared-down interior is the ideal material to summon imaginative French-Asian dishes utilising scavenged fixings that they supernaturally artfully into flawlessly plated dishes.

Grub and Vine

"So, this is Grub and Vine," says chef Matt Manning as he invites us into his bistro on Bree Street. "Small, vibey, legit, honest," he includes his unique Essex accent - a depiction we find to be a ridiculous misrepresentation in the wake of taking a significant piece of our starters: new-season asparagus, ricotta beignet, hen egg, mushroom ketchup, and hazelnuts.

The characterful interiors - troubled substantial floors, avian prints, rattan seats, barometrical hanging lights, and pot plants all over the place - improve the buzzy vibe in the minimal

50-seater. That, and the way that the galley is on show, so diners can watch Matt and his bustling team while they wait for their meal.

Tjing Tjing Torii

You'll find this brightly coloured street-food joint at street level, where the pulsating pace, ultra-cool electro-indie beats, Harajuku-inspired decor and on-the-ball service are the perfect backdrop for flavour-popping, Japanese street food.

Torii serves an array of options, including ramen and yakitori (skewers), rice bowls, tebasaki (chicken wings), and classic Japanese confections (such as mochi truffles with a Tjing Tjing twist and fluffy Japanese cheesecake).

Hemelhuijs

The highly creative seasonal menu is bursting with options, one more delicious than the next. Whet your appetite with a freshly squeezed juice, then settle in for a comforting homemade potato rösti with lightly smoked trout, soft whipped herb cheese and a soft poached egg, or old-fashioned grilled farm-style sausage in a rich tomato smoor with buttered toast.

The Waterside

It is a harbourside eatery at the V&A Waterfront – a light, bright, pared-down space with views and a deck that makes you feel as if you're on a superyacht.

From the unique Japanese-inspired milk bun stack for starters, through a Cape Malay-tinged prawn salad; snap-pea risotto with zucchini and asparagus; grass-fed beef; and exquisitely prepared seabass, to a "treasure chest" of hand-crafted bonbons for a sweet finish. At about R795 for essentially five courses, this is ridiculously good value for money.

Section 6

Ways to Save Money While Visiting Cape Town

Holidays can be costly, yet they don't need to be. There are numerous useful cash-saving tips yet live them up. In a city like Cape Town, with its outside culture, making do with a budget is simple. One of Cape Town's best attractions is nature, where you could go through hours climbing, swimming, sunbathing, or partaking in sports.

Save money with online bookings

Whether you're reserving for events or attractions, there are many discounts for appointments made online. City Touring offers discounts for tickets purchased online — in addition, you get to avoid the line. Most live music venues likewise offer discounts for tickets bought online ahead of time.

Enjoy free (or truly reasonable) activities

What preferred cash saving tip over by not spending it by any stretch of the imagination? Cape Town is a wonderland of free exercise. With vast experiences to be had in mountains, woodland, and the ocean, you could undoubtedly fill an occasion without spending much by any means. Try out a portion of the staggering climbing trails, visit the seashores, go pursuing cascades, or go through a day investigating the parks and gardens all around the city.

Hit the beach

Get outside and appreciate one of Cape Town's delightful seashores for a day of fun without spending a dime. Pack your picnic lunch, a towel, and heaps of sunblock. Go through the day swimming, sunbathing, eating, and meeting local people right at home.

Go wine tasting

Cape Town's grape plantations produce incredibly popular wine, and it's likewise a fabulous method for going through a day without burning through every last dollar. Many wine bequests offer free tastings, and others charge an ostensible expense (for the most part under R50). It's likewise typically the most reasonable method for getting your hands on excellent wine at much lower costs than the alcohol stores. Simply pick a wine course and get exploring!

Make use of discount vouchers

One of the most well-known ways of seeing the city and getting around is the City Touring bus. Numerous courses are taken in the city's greatest attractions, and it's a reasonable method for getting around the city on the off chance that you're hanging around for a couple of days. Make sure to hold tight to your ticket, since it contains discount vouchers for attractions, dinners, visits, and knick-knacks.

Utilise these vouchers to take the expense of your day out way down.

Pay special attention to the restaurant's specials

Consistently in Cape Town, there's a way for feasting for a small part of the normal cost. There are two-for-one specials, cheerful hours, and a wide range of different specials that will permit you to eat like a king on a careful financial plan.

Book flights early and Look out for specials

Flights are many times the greatest drain on funds while going on vacation, however, they needn't bother with them too. Assuming you check consistently for flight deals you're probably going to track down awesome arrangements. It's likewise essential to book your trips as far ahead of time as could be expected, so if you're pondering visiting Cape Town, don't pause! Book your flights now.

Book accommodation wisely

Top season is continuously going to be somewhat pricier, so consider booking your trip for shoulder season (March, April, September, or October) for lower rates. You could likewise come in the colder time of year to exploit the numerous specials on accommodation. Try Airbnb for reasonable self-catering, and decide to remain in additional reasonable regions.

Section 7

Travel cape town on a budget

Situated in the middle of stunning mountains and amazing beaches, you can't beat that! If you're from Europe or North America, your money will go far in South Africa yet assuming that you anticipate remaining in Cape Town for some time, things can begin to add up.

Pick the Right Accommodation

The cost of accommodation changes relying upon the season you're going through Cape Town. At the point when I originally arrived in November (just before peak season), lodging dorm rooms were pretty much as low as $10 however they went up to around $20 as summer drew closer.

If you have any desire to travel to Cape Town on a tight spending plan, hostels are typically your smartest option! So, some of the time, Airbnb can be to some degree reasonable if you're sharing a spot with a couple of individuals. Assuming you're hoping to set aside some cash, you can chip in through Worldpackers! Most lodgings will request a couple of long stretches of work a day in return for a free spot to remain. On the off chance that you do want to work at a hostel, numerous other workers open doors.

Make Your Meals

It could be enticing to order the entirety of your food or eat at restaurants and cafés while you're in Cape Town since it's reasonably a small part of what it would cost at home. While nothing bad can be said about having a couple of dinners out with new companions, you can set aside a Ton of cash on the off chance that you choose to make a few meals from your hostel or Airbnb.

Making breakfast is simple and requires a minimal measure of exertion so that is a decent spot to begin if you don't cook a lot.

Embrace Free Activities

Cape Town is an extraordinary city to visit when you're on a careful budget since there are countless free or modest activities. First off, the first Thursday of every month is known as 'First Thursdays'. Everybody assembles on Bree St and Long St to have drinks and look at craftsmanship displays that are open late. A few galleries even give out free wine which is a plus! It's certainly an unquestionable requirement on the off chance that you're here toward the beginning of the month. From time to time, you'll likewise catch wind of street parties where a segment of Bree St, for instance, will be shut and there are various DJs, live music, and food stands.

Since Cape Town is encircled by mountains, you don't need to go far to do fantastic climbs. Contingent upon where you're remaining, you can stroll to some, including Lion's Head and Kloof Corner. Simply make sure to hike with a mate or in a group, as hiking alone in South Africa is genuinely risky.

Your time in Cape Town is unfinished until you've had sundowners at the beach. Clifton second or Camps Bay is an extraordinary spot to watch the sun go down. There are countless perfect beaches close to the city that likewise make for superb oceanside days with new friends! Llandudno is a piece further (20ish min from the city) and you'd have to arrive by Uber or lease a vehicle yet it merits the mission.

Ultimately, assuming you're into skating, biking, rollerblading, and so forth, you Should look at Promenade Mondays. Everybody meets Monday nights around 6 pm at the Sea Point Contact (parking garage) and afterward, coasts along the promenade until the sun goes down.

Know How to Get Around

The least demanding method for getting around Cape Town is Uber. It's substantially more reasonable than it is in different nations and the vast majority use it to get from one spot to another. Bolt is another choice (that is of time less expensive than Uber).

Section 8

The Ultimate 4-Day Cape Town Itinerary

There are so many countless activities to do and see in Cape Town. 5 days isn't enough, however, it's certainly incredible to begin to expose this astounding city!

Day 1

Bo-Kaap

Start your Cape Town trip with a visit to the brilliant neighbourhood of Bo-Kaap. You could perceive this region with the splendid, bright houses just like a famous Instagram photograph operation, yet it's far beyond that. Bo-Kaap has a rich social legacy. The Malay people who resided here before they were liberated from servitude were not permitted to paint their white houses. So whenever they were liberated, they painted their homes the splendid varieties that you see today!

Invest some energy strolling around these roads. Take a few pictures, visit the small museum, or on the other hand if you have time - take a cooking class with a local Bo-Kaap occupant!

V&A Waterfront

Take a 10-min Uber ride from Bo-Kaap to the famous V&A Waterfront district, which is situated on South Africa's most seasoned harbour. There's dependably a ton happening here. You'll see street entertainers, shops, bars and eateries, a Ferris wheel, and a perspective on famous Table Mountain behind the scenes. All things considered, Stop here for lunch as well as a beverage with a view sitting above the marina! If you have additional time/interest, consider taking a boat tour, going on an outing to Robben Island to find out about Nelson Mandela, or looking at the Nelson Mandela museum.

Dinner at Pot Karma Club

There are numerous elite restaurants in Cape Town, yet Pot Luck Club is one of the most iconic. Situated in the Old Biscuit Mill with perspectives on Table Mountain, this stylish café is shared tapas style and is likewise known for its art mixed drinks. Reserve a spot well ahead of time.

Day 2

Lion's Head Hike

Hiking Lion's Head was one of my #1 recollections of our 5 days in Cape Town. Most people who are visiting Cape Town who believe that they should do a hike pick either Lion's Head or Table Mountain. If you just have time or energy to climb one of them, hike Lion's Head.

You can take a cable car up Table Mountain, yet the best way to get up to Lion's Head is to hike.

It's very much stamped, open all year, and is dog friendly. There are a couple of short stepping stools that everybody should climb, but you can skirt the most troublesome aspect (including chains + staples in the stone as tractions), by taking left at the fork in the path. Anyway, if you are not frightened of levels, I suggest taking the course of the chain up! It's fun.

When you get to the highest point of Lion's Head, you are compensated with 360-degree views of Cape Town, the coast, and Table Mountain. It's shocking!

Breakfast at Nourish'd

After your morning climbs, go to the local juice bar/acai bowl spot "Nourish'd". This adorable spot at the intersection of Kloof Street has astounding acai bowls, smoothies, and other solid breakfast things.

Camp's Bay

Use the remainder of your day unwinding at the beach at Camps Bay. Try things out, partake in the landscape, yet additionally go for a chance to stroll along the central avenue and jump into a portion of the shops, bars, and restaurants.

Dinner and Drinks

Reserve a spot for dinner at Kloof Street House. The food is perfect and the climate is heavenly. Set in a lavishly embellished Victorian house, you can get a table inside to admire the style. Or on the other hand, get a table outside in their nursery region with string lights and lavish plants.

After supper, get some drinks at The Gin Bar. Gin is a staple in South Africa. What better spot to have a gin drink than this little unexpected, yet invaluable treasure of a bar? The Gin Bar feels like a speakeasy - when you show up, you might think you are at some unacceptable location briefly. The outside seems to be a treat shop, yet on the off chance that you stroll in and go the entire way to the back, it opens up into a Mediterranean-style chamber. They have many delectable specialty gin mixed drinks that are a must-try.

Day 3:

Table Mountain

Table Mountain is the flat-topped mountain that is quite often present in your views around Cape Town. It's one of the 7 Natural Miracles of the World! You can't come to Cape Town without adding this spot to your agenda. It's the most popular milestone in South Africa!

Getting to the Top

There are two choices for getting to the top:

- Hiking
- Cable car

Hiking Table Mountain

The climb up to Table Mountain is recorded as decently testing. It's 4.2 miles out and back, with a 3,369ft rise gain. It's a lofty scramble! On the off chance that you need it, you can likewise climb up and bring the cable car down (or the other way around).

Cable car

To take the cable car, you need tickets. You can either purchase online quite a bit early, or purchase in the box office there. It costs about $24 for a ticket to go full circle. There is likewise a choice to purchase a "fastrak" ticket online where you can skirt the line for about twofold the cost.

What to expect at Table Mountain

When you're at the top, there are a couple of short, cleared trails to stroll alongside notices instructing on the set of experiences and nature of Table Mountain. The perspectives up here are unimaginable! There is likewise a little bistro at the top to manoeuvre a dinner or a few drinks before heading down.

It tends to be freezing and breezy at the highest point of Table Mountain, so make a point to wear layers to be ready! Assuming it is ever excessively breezy, they will prevent the cable car from running until the breeze fades away.

Kirstenbosch National Botanical Garden

This botanical garden is known as one of the main 7 radiant professional flower beds on the planet. It's situated on the eastern incline of Table Mountain. The nurseries comprise around 1.3 sections of land loaded up with native plants, including a few intriguing and imperilled species.

Day 4:

Cape Winelands

No trip to Cape Town is finished without visiting the world-renowned Cape Winelands! The views here are staggering, the wine is perfect, and the food is elite.

There are a couple of areas of wine country, yet the two main ones are Stellenbosch and Franschhoek. They are around 30 minutes separated from one another, so you can visit both around the same time assuming that you wish. Stellenbosch is only 50 minutes from the Camp's Bay area of Cape Town, and Franschoek is 1 hour and 15 minutes away.

The drive there from Cape Town is quite simple on the off chance that you have a rental car, but I wouldn't suggest rolling around there for a road trip assuming you will drink. All things considered, pick a road trip visit from one of the nearby operators. This Entire Day Winelands Visit and Tasting is an incredible choice! For $78 you get transportation to/from

Stellenbosch AND Franschhoek, in addition to 3 wine samplings (and a cheddar tasting) included.

Private Trip to Cape Winelands

Assuming you have over 5 days in Cape Town, I energetically suggest spending somewhere around 1 or 2 evenings in the Cape Winelands. The view from the room is shocking. What's more, you're likewise right nearby to Delaire Graff Estate which is known for extraordinary wine and a fantastic restaurant.

Make a point to visit Babylonstoren for breakfast, lunch, or wine sampling on this delightful farm bequest, as well as the honour winning eatery Rust en Vrede for dinner.

Conclusion

Cape Town is the seat of government for the South African Republic. It serves as the provincial capital of the Western Cape. Cape Town, which is situated on Table Bay, has long been a significant regional port.

The Dutch explorer Jan van Riebeeck established the first town in Table Bay for the Dutch East India Company in the 17th century, and it quickly became a stopover for ships travelling the route from Europe to India. Up to the British invasion in 1806, it was sporadically ruled by the Dutch.

It serves as a hub for commerce and culture today.

Enjoy your vacation in Cape Town...

Printed in Great Britain
by Amazon

31149114R00050